AF615187

Presented

to

by

DATE

GOOD MORNING, LORD
Devotions for Boys

William C. Hendricks

BAKER BOOK HOUSE
Grand Rapids, Michigan

First printing, April 1974
Second printing, December 1976
Third printing, October 1979
Fourth printing, September 1981
Fifth printing, September 1982

ISBN: 0-8010-4100-7

Printed in the United States of America

1. STRONG MUSCLES

SCRIPTURE: Psalm 84

Blessed are the men whose strength is in thee, in whose heart are the highways to Zion. Ps. 84:5

You have probably seen a weight-lifting contest. You may have been watching TV when the world champion weight-lifting contest was on. Did you wish your muscles were as strong and big as those of the weight-lifters?

At one time a farmer gave his son a small pig. It weighed only ten pounds. Each day the boy lifted the pig from one side of the fence to the other side so he could more easily clean its pen. As time passed the pig grew, slowly but steadily.

Of course, the day came when the boy could no longer lift the pig over the fence, but the daily exercise had made the boy's muscles much stronger than when he first began.

Perhaps you have a regulation set of weights. If not, you can easily make a set with some pipe, a little cement, and two one-gallon buckets. One thing is certain, however: the weights will do you no good unless you exercise with them.

Growing in your Christian faith takes daily exercise too. Each time you make a decision to tell the truth and to be honest, your spiritual muscles grow stronger.

CHALLENGE: Find one way to strengthen your Christian faith by exercising it today.

2. *WAKE UP! JUMP OUT!*

SCRIPTURE: Genesis 13:1-13

> *So Lot chose for himself all the Jordan valley, . . . Lot dwelt among the cities of the valley and moved his tent as far as Sodom. Gen. 13:11, 12*

What do you know about frogs? Have you ever collected frog eggs or watched them hatch into tadpoles? Soon their tails drop off and they learn to jump instead of swim.

If you should drop a frog into a pan of hot water, it would jump right out. But if you put it in cold water and heated the water gradually, the slow change of temperature wouldn't bother the frog. You could even heat the water to the boiling point, and if you did it slowly enough, the frog wouldn't jump out—it would die instead.

Lot behaved like that. First he chose the Jordan Valley. Then he pitched his tent toward the wicked city of Sodom. In Genesis 19:1 we read that Lot was sitting in the gate of the city. If the angels of the Lord hadn't pulled him away, he would have died there when the city was destroyed.

We sometimes act that same way. If we see or do a little sin, we don't notice it too much. We may repeat that sin with only a little warning from our conscience. Soon we begin to like that sin and, what's worse, we aren't even bothered by more sins and bigger sins that slowly creep into our lives. Is that happening to you?

CHALLENGE: Look at your life—are there sins you have become used to because they grow so slowly you haven't noticed? If so, WAKE UP—JUMP OUT, before it's too late!

3. *SLINGSHOT PRACTICE*

SCRIPTURE: I Samuel 17:40-49

Then he . . . chose five smooth stones from the brook, and put them in his shepherd's bag . . . his sling was in his hand, and he drew near to the Philistine. I Sam. 17:40

King David was once a shepherd boy. He knew what it was to spend many long and lonely nights with his father's flock of sheep on a hillside in Judea.

He knew what it was to be watchful and ready for animals that might attack the lambs of the flock. And part of his readiness was his slingshot.

David must have spent much time practicing —selecting stones and carefully aiming at rocks or other targets over and over until his arm was tired. Over and over, until he could hit the target without fail. If a wild animal came looking for a lamb, it was a good idea to have his slingshot ready.

Later in David's life, his skill with a slingshot was a means of saving God's people. God used the skill of David to overcome the strongest man ever to face Israel's armies.

Which skills has the Lord given you to help His people and build His kingdom?

CHALLENGE: Think of a skill you have and a way you can use it for God today.

4. *DON'T FORGET*

SCRIPTURE: Ecclesiastes 12

Remember also your Creator in the days of your youth, before the evil days come, and the years draw nigh, when you will say, "I have no pleasure in them." Eccles. 12:1

Near a village in India an elephant had just finished his bath. Then he filled his trunk with the dirtiest water he could find in the river and went directly down the road to the open window of a tailor's shop. SWOOSH! He blew the muddy water all over the tailor, for he had not forgotten the time when the tailor had pricked him with a needle as he playfully put his trunk in the window some weeks before. The elephant remembered.

Perhaps you intended to do your homework last night, but a friend came to play. Or maybe a good TV program came on and you forgot all about the lessons you planned to do. Sometimes we forget things our parents ask us to do, such as hanging up our clothes. Many adults make New Year's Day resolutions but find that before January 1 has passed they are already forgotten.

Nations have special days to remember soldiers, sailors, and others who gave their lives for their country. Without these days, citizens might soon forget those who died to keep their country free.

Our Scripture verse tells us to "remember our Creator." This is a reminder we all need. We so easily forget the God who made all things because we are so busy with the things He made.

CHALLENGE: Look around. Open your eyes to the wonderful creation that surrounds you. Remember your Creator!

5. BUILD A MODEL

SCRIPTURE: John 13:4-17

For I have given you an example, that you also should do as I have done to you. John 13:15

You have to work carefully when you build a model. Perhaps you have tried to build a model car or airplane or maybe you have a collection of models.

Inside the box are all of the parts but as yet the model doesn't look much like the picture on the outside. There is one other very important thing in the box and that is the set of directions for putting the model together. Trying to get all of the little parts in the right place is difficult enough. If you didn't have the directions it would be almost impossible.

When you have it finished, you don't have the real automobile or airplane. You have a model that has the same appearance. The better the model is, the more it looks like the real thing.

Long ago in the city of Antioch, the followers of Christ were first called *Christians.* Those who love and serve him today are still called by that name.

What kind of directions did Jesus give for the lives of those who want to be His models, those who follow Him? For one thing, when He washed the feet of His disciples, He said we had to show our love by humbly serving others.

How can you tell if a person is a Christian? It's like looking at a model—the model of a Model-T Ford should look like a real one. The life of a Christian should follow the example, or model, of Christ.

THOUGHT: When others look at your life, can they see you are a Christian? Need help with the model you're building? Check the directions—in the Bible.

6. *BE WISE*

SCRIPTURE: I Kings 3:3-15

> *Happy is the man who finds wisdom, and the man who gets understanding, For the gain from it is better than gain from silver and its profit better than gold. Prov. 3:13, 14*

Scientists tell us there are about one hundred different species of owls. Some of the best known are the snowy owl, the screech owl, and the great horned owl.

If you've been on a campout in the woods and there was an owl in the area, you may have been frightened or awakened with his cry, "Whooo, Whooo."

Many people think of the owl as a symbol of wisdom. When they see a wise person, they may say, "He's wise as an owl!"

The Bible tells us to be wise, to search after wisdom. When Solomon became the King of Israel, God came to him in a dream at night and told Solomon to ask for whatever he wanted. Because Solomon asked for wisdom instead of riches or long life or power over his enemies, God gave him all of the other things as well.

The fear of the Lord is the beginning of wisdom.

CHALLENGE: Search after wisdom—be wise as an owl.

7. CHANGING COLORS

SCRIPTURE: Daniel 3:16-30

> *. . . be it known to you, O king, that we will not serve your gods or worship the golden image which you have set up. Dan. 3:18*

Chameleons are hard to find. They seem to change color. If one is resting on a brown piece of bark, it will look brown. If he moves to a green leaf, his body will take on a green hue so that his enemies will have trouble spotting him. His best defense is to fade into the background.

Standing out from those around you so that you can be easily seen is a daring thing to do. It is easier to be so like the crowd you are with that you won't be noticed.

When King Nebuchadnezzar commanded all of his subjects to bow down to the great golden idol he had made, Daniel's three friends refused. It took a great deal of courage to stand up and to stand alone. The King had them thrown into the fiery furnace because they disobeyed, but God saved them from harm and brought them honor.

Daring to obey God takes courage. It may mean that you stand all alone sometimes. You can't show that you are a Christian and behave like a chameleon at the same time.

CHALLENGE: If you have to stand alone today to show you are a Christian, will you dare, or will you quietly blend into the background of the crowd like a chameleon?

8. MAKE UP YOUR MIND

SCRIPTURE: I Kings 18:20-40

How long will you go limping with two different opinions? If the Lord is God, follow Him; but if Baal, then follow him. I Kings 18:21

Twenty-eight flavors of ice cream and just enough money to buy one cone.

Two interesting programs on TV but both come on at the same time.

Jack invites you to go skating and Jim wants you to go to the ball game.

Life is full of choices! Decisions are sometimes hard and sometimes easy; some are important and others are not.

Elijah asked the people of Israel to make a very important choice. God had just sent fire from heaven. It burned up the offering, the altar, and the water in the trench around it. Would the people now choose Jehovah as their God, or would they continue to follow King Ahab and Queen Jezebel in the worship of Baal?

The people had to decide—they couldn't serve both Jehovah and Baal.

Jesus said, "He that is not for me is against me."

CHALLENGE: Find one way today to show that you have chosen to serve Jesus.

9. *WATCH YOUR TONGUE*

SCRIPTURE: James 3: 3-10

> *But no human being can tame the tongue. . . . with it we bless the Lord and Father, and with it we curse men, who are made in the likeness of God. From the same mouth come blessing and cursing. My brethren, this ought not to be so . . . James 3:8-10*

Parrots are colorful birds. Their beautifully colored plumage and loud squawks make their cages favorite spots at the zoo. Have you ever heard a parrot say, "Hi!" or ask, "How are you today?"

In the story *Treasure Island* a one-legged pirate, Long John Silver, had a parrot that rode everywhere on his shoulder. The parrot would say "pieces of eight," "man overboard" and other sayings he had learned from his years at sea.

A parrot can only repeat what someone else has taught it to say because it doesn't think for itself. It doesn't know whether the words it repeats are good or bad.

Recently when a small boy was asked why he had said something he shouldn't have, he replied, "I didn't say it, my tongue did."

But people aren't parrots. People can think and they express their thoughts in words. We are responsible for the things we say. Matthew 12:36 says, "I tell you on the day of Judgment men will render account for every careless word they utter, for by your words you will be justified and by your words you will be condemned."

CHALLENGE: Don't be a parrot! Don't simply repeat what others say. Be sure your words are pleasing to God.

10. *BETTER THAN A GENERAL*

SCRIPTURE: Judges 11:29-40

He who is slow to anger is better than the mighty, and he who rules his spirit than he who takes a city.
Prov. 16:32

An old fable tells about a race between a hare, or rabbit, and a turtle. The hare ran swiftly and could easily have won, but he was so sure he would win that he stopped to take a nap. While the hare slept, the turtle slowly and steadily trudged on and won the race.

Scientists have learned to use time-lapse photography to take pictures of things that move very slowly. They can take pictures of a slowly opening bud until it becomes a flower. They can measure the slow growth of a tree and the slow erosion of the soil.

Usually we think speed is best. Get a job done quickly; have the mail delivered the same day; get dressed in just a few minutes; take the plane instead of the train; take the car instead of walking. Hurry! Hurry! Hurry!

But there is one thing the Bible tells us to do slowly—be slow to get angry. Hasty words are often not good words. Count to ten before you say an angry word and by that time hopefully you will have had time to realize you shouldn't say it at all.

The text for today says that if you can control your temper, watch your words, and do not get angry easily, you are better than a mighty general who orders many men to capture a city. Think about that . . . better than a General!

CHALLENGE: Think carefully before you speak.

11. *GOING THE RIGHT WAY?*

SCRIPTURE: Jonah 1:1-10

So the captain came and said to him, "What do you mean, you sleeper? Arise, call upon your god! Perhaps the god will give a thought to us, that we do not perish." Jonah 1:6

Recently the newspapers told of a stowaway on an airplane. This young man had hidden in the wheel compartment of the plane. He hoped to fly from Australia to the United States without paying the usual fare. But the plane flew several miles high where the temperature was below zero and he froze to death on the way over.

Stowaways on ships are more common. They slip aboard and hide in the freight compartment or even in a lifeboat until the ship comes to another port.

Jonah wasn't a stowaway. He paid his fare and then he went into the bottom of the boat to sleep. He was awakened by the captain who asked him to get up and to pray that God might save them from the storm.

Jonah was going the wrong way. God had told him to go to preach to the city of Nineveh but Jonah decided to go in the opposite direction to Tarsus.

God's Word tells us clearly the direction to travel in life. Are you headed the right way?

CHALLENGE: Think about your life—Are you going God's Way?

12. *MAN OVERBOARD*

SCRIPTURE: Jonah 1:11-17

So they took up Jonah and threw him into the sea. Jonah 1:15

"Man overboard! Man overboard!" This was a fearful cry in the early days of sailing. It meant that some crew member, perhaps a sailor who was on a high mast working with the ropes and sails, had been blown off into the sea, or someone on the deck had been carried away with a giant wave that washed across the ship. Almost always it meant death for the person who had fallen or was swept into the sea.

When Jonah asked the sailors to throw him into the sea, it must have really surprised them. They didn't want to do this to Jonah. But it was the only way to save the ship and themselves. They prayed that God would forgive them—and they threw Jonah overboard.

Two miracles followed—the storm immediately stopped its raging, and God put a great fish there to swallow Jonah and bring him back to land.

God used a most unusual and uncomfortable way to turn Jonah around and set him in the right direction again. In Old Testament times, when Israel would turn to false religions, often God would send enemies so the people would turn back to Him. In the New Testament (John 15:1, 2), Jesus said He was the vine and we are the branches and "every branch that beareth fruit, he purgeth it, that it may bring forth more fruit." Today God may still send us troubles to make us depend more on Him.

THOUGHT: Do our troubles draw us closer to Jesus?

13. NEWS FLASH!

SCRIPTURE: Jonah 3

> *Now Nineveh was an exceedingly great city, three days' journey in breadth. Jonah began to go into the city. . . . And he cried, "Yet forty days, and Nineveh shall be overthrown!" Jonah 3:3, 4*

Have you ever watched TV when the program was suddenly interrupted by some important news flash? Maybe it was a tornado warning or an important international crisis. News spreads quickly today. Radios even tell us when there has been an accident or where there is a fire so that we may avoid traffic jams.

Before radio or TV was invented, newspapers would print the news and newsboys would stand on the street corners shouting, "Extra! Extra! Read all about it!"

Jonah the prophet went into the great city of Nineveh with important news. He walked through the city, crying: "Yet forty days and the city will be overthrown!" Can you imagine the reaction of those who heard him?

The people who heard Jonah told others. The news traveled fast and soon the tidings reached the ears of the king. The king didn't laugh or think it was a joke. Instead he asked his people to repent, to leave their evil ways, and to turn to God in the hope that God would spare them.

SOMETHING TO THINK ABOUT: What is the best thing to do if "bad news" comes to you today?

14. *HAVE A GOOD DAY!*

SCRIPTURE: Jonah 4

Then Jonah went out of the city and sat to the east of the city, and made a booth for himself there. He sat under it in the shade, till he should see what would become of the city. Jonah 4:5

"Good morning!"
"Good night!"
"Happy Birthday!"
"Happy New Year!"
"Merry Christmas!"

All of these are good wishes we say to others. We hope our friends will have joy or success or blessing.

It is easy to say nice things to someone, but it is harder to really mean them, especially if that person has nicer things or perhaps more things than we do. In fact, we may secretly hope he has a bad morning or an unhappy new year instead.

Jonah was like that. He was a lonely, penniless prophet who had proclaimed that the city would be destroyed. Now he wanted to see it happen.

Instead of destroying the city, God showed His love by sparing the city, for the people had listened to the warning and repented. God sent a plant to shade Jonah. God used the plant to teach Jonah that he ought to love the people of Nineveh too.

PRAYER: Lord, help me to love others in the same way that You have loved me. Amen.

15. OVER THE HURDLES

SCRIPTURE: Philippians 4:10-13

I can do all things in Him who strengthens me. Phil. 4:13

Hurdle races are held on the same smooth track as the regular racing events of a track meet. There is one big difference, however. Wooden frames, thirty-two inches high for the low hurdle race, and thirty-nine inches high for the high hurdles, are placed about every twenty yards along the track.

These hurdles make the race much harder than running along the smooth, even track.

The Christian life has hurdles too. Sometimes they are low and easy to overcome. Sometimes they are high and difficult. Sometimes they are far apart and at other times quite close together.

Sometimes these problems cause the Christian to slow down in his progress on the road of life; sometimes they are so high or difficult, he may feel like quitting the race. But with each burden God gives strength. With each trial God gives grace.

Every hurdle that we overcome today will give us strength and courage to meet tomorrow's hurdles.

PRAYER: Lord, give me the strength I need today to face any hurdles that might block my way as I seek to do Your will. Amen.

16. *WIN THE RACE*

SCRIPTURE: Hebrews 12:1-4

. . . let us also lay aside every weight, and sin which clings so closely, and let us run with perseverance the race that is set before us. Heb. 12:1

The starting official pulled the trigger. With the sound of the gun, the runners were off. The first race was the one-hundred-yard dash. The boys in the race used every ounce of their strength, for the distance was short. Later, when the runners in the mile race started, they began at a steady, even pace, saving their greatest strength for the final lap around the track, when the finish was near. A runner wears only light clothing because he doesn't want any weight to slow down his running.

Sometimes events in our lives are like the one-hundred-yard dash, and sometimes they are like the one-mile race. There will be times that require you to use all your strength and energy to reach a short-term goal. At other times you may have to work a long time to reach a goal. There is always the steady, life-long race of doing your best in God's service.

In the days of the apostle Paul, runners would wear weights on their feet when they practiced. Then in the race itself their feet would feel lighter and they could run faster.

CHALLENGE: If there are things that are weighing you down, lay them aside so you can better serve Jesus.

17. HOPE

SCRIPTURE: Lamentations 3:21-24

May the God of hope fill you with all joy and peace in believing, so that by the power of the Holy Spirit you may abound in hope. Rom. 15:13

"I hope the weather will be nice for the picnic!"
"I hope we will win!"
"I hope I can go!"
"I hope so!"

We often use the word *hope.* It means to wish, to expect, to desire, to trust. If men are lost in a boat at night, or in a storm, they might send up a flare with the hope that someone would see it and rescue them.

"Hope" is the name given to a large ship. You may have read about the large red cross painted on its sides. There are modern operating rooms and hospital wards on board. This ship brings hope to many people in the world, for it brings medical know-how to far-off places.

Hope is something we all need. When we are unhappy, we hope that soon things will be better. And the hope we have makes it easier to bear our trouble. When people have no hope, they fall deeper into discouragement and despair.

God doesn't need to hope. He has the power to control all things and He knows the future as well as the past. Because God doesn't need to hope, we can hope in God.

CHALLENGE: Place your hope in God for He holds the whole world in His hand.

18. SECRET SERVICE

SCRIPTURE: Nehemiah 2:1-8

Now I was cupbearer to the king. Neh. 2:1

The US Secret Service provides body guards for important government leaders. Whenever the President goes on a trip, or even when he goes to a program or a ball game, he is accompanied by armed guards. If someone would try to shoot the President, one of the Secret Service men would quickly stand in front of him. If necessary, that man would die to protect the life of the President.

Long ago Nehemiah was something like a Secret Service man. He was the cupbearer for King Artaxerxes. Nehemiah had to taste the wine before the king drank of it to be sure that it was not poisoned. Nehemiah had one of the most important positions in the kingdom. He was the king's most trusted servant. But Nehemiah's important position did not make him happy. God's temple in Jerusalem was in ruins and he longed to return and rebuild it.

Nehemiah gained the permission of the king to return to Jerusalem. He crossed rivers and deserts and faced many hardships along the way. When he got to Jerusalem, the rubble of the old buildings had to be removed and the city walls and the temple had to be completely rebuilt.

Rebuilding the temple so the people could again worship in the house of God was one of the greatest joys of Nehemiah's life.

THOUGHT: How much does the church mean to you? How can you tell?

19. *HUMPTY DUMPTY'S FALL*

SCRIPTURE: Acts 20:7-12

> *A young man named Eutychus was sitting in the window. He sank into a deep sleep as Paul talked still longer; and being overcome by sleep, he fell down from the third story and was taken up dead. But Paul went down and bent over him, and embracing him said, "Do not be alarmed, for his life is in him." Acts 20:9, 10*

One of the nursery rhymes you learned, probably at home or in kindergarten, was about Humpty Dumpty. Humpty Dumpty was an egg. At the beginning of the poem, he was sitting on a wall. He was probably smiling and dangling his legs over the edge in the pictures you saw. But then he fell. CRASH! SPLASH! And nobody—not even all the king's horses and all the king's men—could put poor Humpty Dumpty together again.

In Acts 20:9 we read about a young man who was sitting high up in a church window. The apostle Paul was preaching and as the sermon grew longer, Eutychus fell asleep. He fell off the window ledge and down to his death three floors on the ground below. When Paul prayed to the King of kings, the life of Eutychus was restored.

Sin has made our lives to be as broken as Humpty Dumpty's shell. We want to do wrong things. We are unhappy, we are mean to others, and nothing satisfies us. All the kings of earth cannot help to give us a new and happier life. But Jesus Christ, the King of kings, can. He makes us whole, gives us happy hearts, and helps us to love others.

CHALLENGE: Ask Jesus to remove the cracks and broken spots in your life.

20. HARD WORKERS

SCRIPTURE: Proverbs 6:6-11

Go to the ant, O sluggard; consider her ways, and be wise. Prov. 6:6

If you have ever watched an anthill, you know what a busy place it is! Some of the ants are at work enlarging the tunnels that make up the colony. They haul the extra dirt outside and add it to their hill.

Other members of the ant community care for the young. They may even carry the larvae out to enjoy the sunshine on a warm day and then carry them back into the tunnels again.

Tiny ants can carry heavy loads. If you watch carefully, you may see an ant carrying a stone several times his own size. Someone has estimated that if a man were as strong as an ant, in proportion to his size, he could lift one hundred twenty tons.

Some ants serve as soldiers to defend the colony against invading ants. They may attack another colony and capture some slaves to work for them.

Certain types of tropical ants can actually sew. They stitch leaves together to make nests in trees. They use their own larvae for the needles. As they force the larvae through a leaf with their strong jaws, the web of the larvae becomes the thread to hold the leaves together.

In an ant colony there is no time for laziness. In the Book of Proverbs Solomon tells us to look at the ants. By watching them, we can learn to use our time wisely.

CHALLENGE: Check to see if your work habits are as good as those of the ants.

21. CLEAN HANDS

SCRIPTURE: Psalm 24

He that hath clean hands shall be stronger and stronger. Job 17:9

If you were playing football and your parents called you for supper, one of them might say, "Be sure to wash your hands before you come to the table." If the playing field was wet and muddy, they might insist that you take a bath.

Tiny babies and patients in a hospital are usually given a bath every morning.

Why all this worry about a little dirt? What's so important about cleanliness?

A French scientist named Pasteur learned that germs in milk could be killed by heating it. When Dr. Anton van Leeuwenhoek discovered the microscope, many germs could be seen for the first time. Today scientists are studying viruses that are so small not even the best microscope is strong enough to make them visible. Germs and viruses that produce disease grow rapidly in dirt.

But when the Bible talks about "clean hands" in our verse for today, it is talking about keeping our hands clean from evil deeds; about not getting them dirty by doing sinful things.

CHALLENGE: Practice good cleanliness habits for the sake of good health, but—more important—keep your hands clean from doing wrong.

22. *LIE DETECTORS*

SCRIPTURE: Acts 5:1-6

You shall not steal, nor deal falsely, nor lie to one another. Lev. 19:11

You've probably heard of a lie detector. It is a machine used by the police or by a judge in court to determine if a person is telling the truth. Wires from the lie detector machine are fastened to the arms of the witness. If he is telling the truth, the indicator on the machine will be steady and even. But if he tells a lie when he answers a question, the indicator will show irregular signals.

The machine measures the heartbeat, the blood pressure, and the amount of perspiration of the witness. All of these things change when a person tells a lie. You can't hide a lie from the machine even though you try very hard to act like you are telling the truth.

Sometimes if we tell the truth and no one will believe us, we wish we could take a lie detector test to prove we are not lying. Usually when we lie, we are glad there is no lie detector attached to our arm.

God doesn't need a lie detector to know when we are telling the truth and when we are not.

After Naaman the Syrian had been healed of his leprosy, he wanted to give rich gifts to Elisha. When Elisha refused, his servant, Gehazi, followed Naaman and lied to get the gifts for himself. He hid the gifts and when Elisha asked him where he had been, Gehazi lied. But God knew the truth and Gehazi received the leprosy of Naaman in punishment for those lies.

CHALLENGE: Be sure that everything you say is really true.

23. QUILLS OR KINDNESS

SCRIPTURE: Ephesians 4:25-31

> *And be kind to one another, tenderhearted, forgiving one another, as God in Christ forgave you. Eph. 4:32*

Porcupines are strange animals. They eat mostly small plants and bark for food. They grow to be about three feet long and are able to climb trees easily because of their sharp claws.

But the strangest thing about a porcupine is its quills. People used to think that a porcupine could shoot its quills at its enemies, but this is not so. The porcupine will slap his enemies with his strong tail. And when he does, the sharp, barbed quills are driven into the enemy. If anything comes to attack him, he can roll up into a ball and no one will want to touch him for fear of being stuck with a quill.

Not very many people would want a porcupine for a pet or would even want to be near one.

Some people are like porcupines. They seem to bristle and harm everyone who comes near them. They may use sharp words or unkind deeds as their quills. No one likes to be near them because anyone who tries to be friendly ends up getting hurt.

The Bible tells us not to be like porcupines. Instead of sending out sharp quills of unkindness or bitterness toward those around us, we are to be as kind as Jesus was. Even on the night when He was betrayed in the Garden of Gethsemane, He healed the ear of one of those who had come out to seize and crucify Him.

CHALLENGE: Don't be a porcupine! Don't let any mean quills escape to hurt others. Instead, go out of your way to show kindness to everyone you can.

24. *TEAM WORK WINS*

SCRIPTURE: I Corinthians 12:12-30

The eye cannot say to the hand, "I have no need of you." I Cor. 12:21

Football is a great sport. The players must be in top physical condition so their muscles can react quickly. The runner must be able to decide in a split second if he should turn right or left. The quarterback must call the signals and pass the ball accurately. The blocker must hold his line against the force of the opposing team.

Planning the strategy of the next play in the huddle and carrying it out successfully is really exciting.

The work of Christians in God's kingdom is a lot like playing a football game. The members of the team must be in strong spiritual condition because the contest with the forces of evil will demand their best efforts. When Christians gather together on Sunday, that is a great deal like a "huddle." Here the plan of God for Christians is made plain through the preaching of His Word. Here the team members get strength and instruction for the push toward the goal of winning others for Christ. The work of the devil must be strongly and firmly blocked and the members of his team pushed steadily back.

A single football player couldn't win the game by himself. The blockers open the way for the man who is carrying the ball; one man passes, another receives the pass. Teamwork wins the game.

CHALLENGE: Talk to another Christian; plan with another Christian; work with another Christian to win others for Christ.

25. LILIES DON'T WORRY

SCRIPTURE: Matthew 6:25-34

> *Consider the lilies of the field, how they grow, they neither toil nor spin; yet I tell you, even Solomon in all his glory was not arrayed like one of these. Matt. 6:28-29*

Spring is a beautiful time of the year—roadsides are yellow with dandelions—bees are busy in patches of white clover—buttercups brighten shady spots along the trails in the woods—wild flowers of many kinds seem to bloom in the most unexpected places.

In Palestine where Jesus lived, one of the most common wild flowers is the lily. It is about the size of a daisy and has a black center—quite different from our Easter lily or calla lily or lily of the valley. Instead it has petals that are bright scarlet—so beautiful that Jesus said they were more gorgeous than King Solomon in his royal robes.

Jesus used these delicate flowers to teach a lesson. The lilies teach us to trust our Heavenly Father. Blossoms have short lives. Palestine lilies last for only about three weeks. Jesus wanted us to learn that if God provided the rain and the sun for flowers that fade away so soon, He could surely be trusted to care for us.

"Consider the lilies—how they grow," said Jesus. They couldn't push themselves up into the air. They could only depend on God for everything they needed.

CHALLENGE: Think of the many ways that God uses to provide for your needs.

26. SEA CREATURES

SCRIPTURE: Nehemiah 9:6-15

> *Thou art the Lord, thou alone; thou hast made heaven, the heaven of heavens, with all their host, the earth and all that is on it, the seas and all that is in them; and thou preservest them all. Neh. 9:6*

A trip to the ocean is exciting for many reasons. It may be just the place for a cooling swim on a hot summer day. It may be great for boating and water skiing or a picnic. You may like to go exploring and gathering driftwood or shells. But one of the most exciting things you can do at the seashore is to discover how many tiny creatures live there.

Sea anemones, shaped and colored like beautiful flowers, can be found fastened in the crevices of rocks. They wait patiently for the tide to come in and to bring them the food they need to survive.

Starfish of many kinds and colors from deep purple to bright gold are uncovered as the tide flows out. When you try to pull one off a rock, you find he is fastened with dozens of tiny suction cups.

You may turn over a rock and the crabs under it scurry to find another hiding place. You look at the rock and there are living barnacles and other tiny shelled creatures fastened to it.

How many ocean creatures have you seen? Octopuses, sand dollars, clams, oysters, sea horses —these are only a few of the more familiar ones. But all of those you know about and all of those you don't know about depend on God who "preserves them all."

CHALLENGE: Take time to think of all the creatures that live in the sea and praise God for caring for them.

27. WHEN GOD SPEAKS

SCRIPTURE: I Samuel 3:2-14

Speak, for thy servant hears. I Sam. 3:10

Samuel's parents had prayed for a child and God answered their prayer by giving them a son.

When Samuel was still a small boy, they brought him to Eli, the high priest. Samuel lived with Eli and worked for him in the temple.

One night when God first called, "Samuel, Samuel" little Samuel got up and hurried to Eli. But Eli hadn't called.

God called a second time and a third time. Each time Samuel thought it was Eli calling. Only after this happened the third time did Eli realize that it was God calling to Samuel. When Samuel answered God, he was told what trouble would soon come to the house of Eli and to Israel.

God doesn't speak to us today by means of a voice in the night. He doesn't just speak to one selected person like He spoke to Samuel. Instead His voice is plainly open to us in the Bible.

The Bible is the world's best-selling book. Almost every person in our country has a copy. Many families have two or three. You probably have your very own copy.

Be like Samuel, listen and hear what God says.

CHALLENGE: Listen!

28. FLY INTO THE WIND

SCRIPTURE: Matthew 14:22-35

For the wind was against them. Matt. 14:24

This Bible passage gives us a picture of the disciples in their boat on the Sea of Galilee. They were rowing hard to get to the other side, but a strong wind came up and they seemed to be making no progress at all. They must have been very tired, worried, and discouraged. The wind was against them.

Running into the wind is harder than running when the wind is behind your back pushing you along. Life is easier too when there are no troubles or discouragements. But there are times when facing into the wind is important.

Have you watched planes taking off at the airport? If you look at the wind sock, you can tell they are taking off into the wind to help them fly easier and gain altitude more quickly.

If you have tried to fly a kite by running with the wind behind you, you know it doesn't work. But when you turn around and face the wind, the kite quickly rises high above the houses and trees. The harder the wind blows, the higher the kite rises to the very end of your string.

Troubles and discouragements affect people that same way—they may blow some people down and keep them down. But if people turn around and face the problem and with God's help rise above it, they will be stronger than they were before the trouble came.

CHALLENGE: Be an airplane—face into the wind and rise above the trouble or discouragement you may have.

29. LIVING WITH BROTHERS

SCRIPTURE: Genesis 37:1-11

> *. . . Joseph brought an ill report of them to their father. Gen. 37:2*

They called him a "dreamer." His father gave him a coat of many colors. He was sold as a slave into Egypt but later he became a ruler of the land. Do you know who that could be?

Yes, it was Joseph. He was his father's favorite son, but his brothers hated him. When Jacob sent Joseph out to see how his brothers were getting along with the flocks of sheep, they sold him as a slave to some Midianites who were on their way to Egypt. Then they tricked their father Jacob into believing Joseph had been killed by some wild animal.

How did Joseph feel about all this? Did he wish he had not told his father about his brother's evil deeds?

Getting along with your brothers is sometimes a hard task. This is especially true if they do something you know is wrong. Should you tell your parents? Will your brother be angry with you if you do?

Jesus gave us the answer in Matthew 18:15-17. "If your brother sin against you, go and tell him his fault between you and him alone. If he listens to you you have gained your brother." After we have tried our best ourselves to help him and if he still refuses to listen, then said Jesus, we are to go to others.

CHALLENGE: If you see others doing things that are sinful—try to do something about it—begin by talking to them.

30. DON'T FORGET THE STAMP

SCRIPTURE: John 14:1-15

. . . if you ask anything in my name, I will do it.
John 14:14

Before you mail a letter you must address it; that is, you need to write on the envelope the name of the person who is to get the letter and where he lives. The name should be written clearly. The house number, the name of the street, city and state must be given. Even the ZIP code should be included. Letters that do not have complete addresses usually end in the dead-letter office of the postal department.

But letters still need something else—a stamp. The money you pay for the stamp pays the cost of delivering the letter.

Our prayers are a great deal like letters. They must be addressed to the right Person. Jesus taught us to pray to Our Father who is in heaven. We send our messages to Him because He hears and can answer our requests.

But our prayers must have a stamp—the stamp of Jesus Christ. He has paid the cost. For His sake God hears and answers the prayers we send to Him.

If we would pray in our own name, or in the name of some other person, our requests would not be delivered. They would be like the envelopes that end in the dead-letter office.

THOUGHT: When you pray, don't forget to add the stamp: "In Jesus Name" for this will guarantee its delivery.

31. THE BEST FOOD

SCRIPTURE: John 6:31-40

Jesus said to them, "I am the bread of life; he who comes to me shall not hunger, and he who believes in me shall never thirst. John 6:35

Do you love to eat? Many people have tried to set records for eating the most food at once. Philip Yazdizk of Chicago ate 77 hamburgers at one meal. Paul Hughes, age 13, ate 39 peanut butter and jam sandwiches. Still others try to see how fast they can eat, for example, Steven Nel, age 30, ate 50½ bananas in ten minutes. Sian Davis with his team of three men ate 100 yards of spaghetti in 53 seconds.

Good food and enough food are real blessings. We pray for this in the Lord's Prayer when we say, "Give us this day our daily bread."

The food we eat keeps us alive and well and makes it possible for us to grow. But the Bible teaches that "man cannot live by bread alone" (Matt. 4:4).

Our souls need food, too. The Bible is food for the soul. We must read it and study it regularly if our faith is to grow.

CHALLENGE: Compare your prayer and Bible study habits to your eating habits. Are you feeding your soul as well as your body?

32. *STARLINGS TAKE OVER*

SCRIPTURE: Matt. 13:3-9, 18-23

Other seeds fell upon thorns, and the thorns grew up and choked them. Matt. 13:7.

There are about eighty-six hundred different species of birds. The largest is the ostrich of North Africa which grows to be about 9 feet tall, weighs up to 345 pounds, but cannot fly. The smallest is the bee hummingbird of Cuba. It has a wing span of about one inch and weighs about 1/18th of an ounce.

The starling is believed to be the most common wild bird. Almost everyone has seen a starling. Well over a billion starlings are living in the world today.

If a few starlings come to live in your backyard, they will multiply rapidly. Soon they will chase away the swallows, the cardinals, the robins, and even the blue jays. The starlings may take over the whole neighborhood.

When Jesus told a parable about a sower, He said that some of the seed started growing but soon the thorns grew up and crowded out the plants. Jesus explained to His disciples that the thorns or weeds were bad things that people did, or wanted, or worried about.

Bad things can crowd out good things.

Bad deeds can crowd out good deeds in the same way that weeds can crowd out the good plants in your garden.

Bad thoughts can crowd out good thoughts in the same way that starlings can crowd out cardinals or wrens from your backyard.

CHALLENGE: When you see a starling or a weed, think about your life—are bad things crowding out good things?

33. SOMETHING PRECIOUS

SCRIPTURE: I Samuel 3:1-9

. . . the word of the Lord was rare in those days. I Sam. 3:1

How many Bibles do you have in your home? Two? Three? Some homes today have several copies of different versions of the Bible. The Gideons and The American Bible Society, and some church groups give copies of the Bible away free of charge.

Bibles are placed in motel rooms; they are given to members of the armed forces, and to people who are locked in prison. Small paperback copies of the New Testament can be bought for less than a dollar.

Long ago in the days of Samuel this was not so. People didn't have books. Instead, prophets brought God's Word to the people. The people knew God's Word was precious for it was very rare. They were eager to hear it.

During the Middle Ages monks would spend years carefully copying the books of the Bible. When the printing press was invented, the first book printed was the Bible. A few of these first printed Bibles are still in existence and in 1970 a rare-book collector paid $2,500,000 for a copy. This book was precious to him because it was so old, not because it was a Bible.

The Bible is precious to us today because it is God's Holy Word. It tells us the way of salvation. It helps us to know God's will for our lives.

QUESTION: How precious is the Bible to you? How can you tell?

34. NOT LIKE LIGHTNING

SCRIPTURE: II Peter 1:5-9

> *. . . make every effort to supplement your faith with virtue, and virtue with knowledge, and knowledge with self-control. . . . II Peter 1:5, 6a*

Lightning is electricity out of control. Lightning has tremendous power. A flash of lightning travels up to 1000 miles per second and may have a temperature of up to 30,000 degrees.

Lightning often starts great forest fires. Even a small flash may split a tree from top to bottom. Lightning can easily kill a herd of cattle or a flock of sheep. It has even killed people who have taken shelter under a tree in a storm. Electricity that is not properly controlled is very dangerous and sometimes deadly.

All useful electric energy is under control. It follows power lines set up for this purpose and is turned on and off with switches.

Our energy needs control as well. If we behave in an uncontrolled way, our energy will do little good, and may even cause damage. Your mind is the control center.

The Bible tells us that we are to exercise self-control. Cain let his anger get out of control and he killed his brother Abel. We are also in danger of losing our self-control under certain conditions. If you think you're losing self-control, STOP! Count to ten or even a hundred before you do an unkind deed. Bite on your tongue before you say an unkind word. Unclench those fists. Run around the house—or around the block if you are really angry. Bring yourself back under control.

CHALLENGE: Don't be a *wild,* useless flash of lightning! Show your power by exercising *your* self-control.

35. THE GOLDEN SPIKE

SCRIPTURE: I Timothy 2:1-6

> *For there is one God, and there is one mediator between God and men, the man Christ Jesus, who gave himself as a ransom for all. . . . I Tim. 2:5, 6*

Gold is a very precious metal. It is used for money and banking, for fine jewelry, and for filling teeth. But did you ever hear of a golden railroad spike?

When the early railroad companies began, there were railroad tracks only in the eastern part of the United States. The companies wanted a track that would go all the way to California.

One building crew started in the west and one in the east. Mile after mile they moved closer together over the rivers, mountains, and plains. On May 10, 1869, in Utah, the two crews finally met. A golden spike was used to join the two ends together. The track was completed and trains could run from one coast to the other. The separated ends had to be brought together.

People are separated from God by sin. We can't build a track to reach God. God built a track or bridge for us to use. Not half of the track, but the whole thing. He gave us His own Son. Like the golden spike that tied the two ends together, Jesus Christ, our Mediator, brings man and God together. Through His shed blood He ties us together for all eternity.

The track is completed. The switches are open. The ticket is paid for. The train is ready. But we must still get on board.

CHALLENGE: Are you on God's track? Don't wait, you may miss the train!

36. LITTLE BUT LARGE

SCRIPTURE: Mark 12:41-44

> *And a poor widow came, and put in two copper coins, which make a penny. And he called his disciples to him, and said to them, "Truly, I say to you, this poor widow has put in more than all those who are contributing to the treasury." Mark 12:42, 43*

Do you hope some day to do great things for the Lord? Like Paul who brought the gospel to Rome? Or Daniel who went to the lion's den rather than stop praying?

I hope you can some day. But the Bible tells us that little things are important too. When the widow put just a few small copper coins in the offering, Jesus noticed and said it was a great gift because she gave all she had.

The Wrigley Chewing Gum Company owns a large skyscraper in Chicago. Gum sells for about a penny a stick. The company must have sold a lot of gum before it had enough money to pay for such a tall building. Many little things soon add up to something big.

Little drops of water,
Little grains of sand;
Make the mighty ocean,
And the pleasant land.

Each little drop of water could easily say, "Well, I'm not big enough to do anything". . . but when all the drops are put together, they make the "mighty ocean."

Don't wait until you are able to do some big thing for the Lord. Show your love to Him by starting on the little things you can do.

CHALLENGE: Find some "little thing" you can do for Jesus.

37. WOLF! WOLF!

SCRIPTURE: I John 3:11-18

> *But if any one has the world's goods and sees his brother in need, yet closes his heart against him, how does God's love abide in him? Little children, let us not love in word or speech but in deed and in truth. I John 3:17, 18*

An old fable tells about a boy who had the job of tending sheep. He would get lonely as he sat on the hillside by himself. One day he had the idea of calling, "Wolf! Wolf!" so that the men of the village would quickly come to help protect the sheep.

He tried his plan and it worked well. The people of the village came but there was no wolf. Later when a wolf really did come, he cried for help again. But this time everyone thought he was only pretending again and they didn't come.

Pretending can be fun but it can also get us into trouble. Judas Iscariot pretended to love Jesus in the Garden of Gethsemane when he betrayed Him with a kiss. Ananias and Sapphira pretended to give all their money to the church when they had already kept out some for themselves. They fell dead at Peter's feet for lying to the Holy Spirit.

Our passage today tells us not just to pretend we love others but to show we love them by our deeds.

THOUGHT: Is your love for others real? How can you tell?

38. PAINTING BY NUMBERS

SCRIPTURE: Luke 10:25-37

> *And he answered, "You shall love the Lord your God with all your heart, and with all your soul, and with all your strength, and with all your mind; and your neighbor as yourself." Luke 10:27*

Painting by numbers is fun. Many people, young and old, enjoy it. You can go into almost any hobby shop or toy store and buy a kit that contains several pictures and many small containers of paint.

The pictures are all divided into small areas and each area has a number. If you follow the directions, take the paint from the small cans and brush it carefully in the correct area, you will end up with a beautiful picture.

God has given us a set of directions for our lives. These directions are found in the Bible. If we follow them carefully we will have lives that are beautiful before Him.

Such a life is filled with JOY.

J stands for Jesus.
O stands for others
Y stands for yourself.

If you think of Jesus first, others second, and yourself last, you will have a life that is beautiful, that is filled with joy.

THOUGHT: What kind of picture are you painting with your life? Step back and take a look. How does it look to you? How does it look to others? How does it look to God? Read the directions again.

39. POISONOUS MUSHROOMS

SCRIPTURE: I Kings 22:13-23

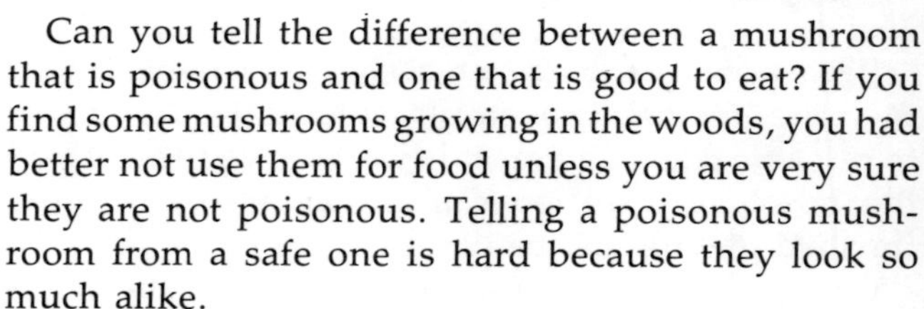

. . . for even Satan disguises himself as an angel of light. II Cor. 11:14

Can you tell the difference between a mushroom that is poisonous and one that is good to eat? If you find some mushrooms growing in the woods, you had better not use them for food unless you are very sure they are not poisonous. Telling a poisonous mushroom from a safe one is hard because they look so much alike.

"Safe" mushrooms are grown on farms. One of the largest mushroom farms in the world is in an old limestone mine in Pennsylvania. Here 900 employees work in underground tunnels about 110 miles long. This farm produces 32 million pounds of "safe" mushrooms each year.

Telling the truth from what is not true is often difficult, too. When Satan first tempted Eve to sin, he made a lie sound like the truth.

Today the devil still tries to fool us by making wrong seem right and right seem wrong. He tries hard to make us say things that are false in a way that makes them sound true. That's his plan. He wants to look harmless when he really is very dangerous. To be fooled by the devil is much more serious than to be fooled by a mushroom.

PRAYER: Lord, help us to be able to tell the difference between that which is good and that which is bad. Help us to believe and to say only that which is really true. Amen.

40. *LIKE A JIGSAW PUZZLE*

SCRIPTURE: Revelation 21:10-25

> *They shall hunger no more, neither thirst any more; . . . For the Lamb in the midst of the throne will be their shepherd, and he will guide them to springs of living water; and God will wipe away every tear from their eyes. Rev. 7:16, 17*

Jigsaw puzzles can be a real challenge, especially if there are 100, 300, or even 1,000 pieces. When you try to put a puzzle together, it helps to have the cover of the box handy so you can check to see what the finished picture will be like.

One day when a mother was shopping, she saw a jigsaw puzzle on the bargain counter. The box had been destroyed but all of the pieces were supposed to be there in a brown bag. She bought the puzzle for her two boys who loved to work them. As they began to fit the pieces together, they wondered if any pieces were missing and what the finished picture would be like.

Trying to learn what heaven is like is something like that. God's Word gives us many of the pieces, but not nearly all of them. We know it will be joyful there. We know we will see Jesus there. We know there will be no sorrow, or sickness, or pain. We have enough pieces to know that the whole picture will be more beautiful than we can even imagine.

When we get to heaven all the things we don't understand now will be clear to us. All the pieces will be there and they will fit together.

PRAYER: Help me to be happy, Heavenly Father, with the pieces of information I have about heaven. Help me to look forward to the day when I can see it in all of its beauty. Amen.

41. A HUNGRY LION

SCRIPTURE: I Peter 5:5-11

Be sober, be watchful. Your adversary the devil prowls around like a roaring lion, seeking some one to devour. I Peter 5:8

Man-eating lions are rare. In parts of Africa where lions are common, they live by killing and eating other animals. When they hunt, they hunt only for the food they need to eat. When other animals sense that a lion is near, they will usually run for their lives or try to hide. They don't want to be the lion's next meal.

Sometimes, however, a lion turns into a man-eater. Once he has come to a village and killed a native, he learns it is much easier to hunt a person than an animal so he will do so again and again.

If a man-eating lion comes near a village, fear fills the hearts of everyone. The warriors must kill him to protect their families. They form a large circle in the bush around the area where they think the lion is. Some of the warriors hide. The other warriors begin to close the circle, all the while shouting and beating loudly on their drums. The noise frightens the lion and he runs toward the hidden warriors who have their spears ready.

The Bible says the devil is like a roaring, hungry lion. The devil isn't afraid of us but he is afraid of God's Word. When the devil tempted Jesus, Jesus used the sword of the Spirit when He said, "It is written . . ."

God's Word is still the sword of the Spirit. It is the strongest weapon God gives us for our fight against the Evil One. With it we can overcome.

THOUGHT: The devil trembles when he sees
The weakest Christian on his knees.

42. *OLD FAITHFUL*

SCRIPTURE: Luke 16:10-13

He who is faithful in a very little is faithful also in much. . . . Luke 16:10

"Old Faithful" geyser has a very good name. You may have read about how it has erupted faithfully on a very regular schedule for many, many years. If you have visited Yellowstone National Park, you have probably seen the sign that tells you just when it will next send up its huge cloud of hot water and steam.

Faithfulness is important. A faithful bus driver is always on time. He doesn't stay home because it is raining or because it is too hot. Day after day, month after month, he is faithful to the work he has to do.

A mother who is faithful to her family doesn't take good care of them one day and forget about them the next day. No, she cares for them regularly, year after year.

God wants us to serve Him faithfully. He is pleased if we think of Him and worship Him in church on Sunday. But He wants us to be faithful to Him during the rest of the week as well.

If we are careful to honor God while we are at home with our parents, but forget about Him when we are out with our friends, our faithfulness needs strengthening.

PRAYER: Dear God, when we are tempted to serve someone or something else instead of You, or when in our weakness we forget about You, draw us close to Yourself and keep us faithful to You only. Amen.

43. LIKE A BULLDOG

SCRIPTURE: Revelation 2:8-11

Be faithful unto death, and I will give you the crown of life. Rev. 2:10

Have you ever seen an English bulldog? Perhaps you have seen a picture of one. If you have, you will remember how his head seems to be too big for his body. His square bottom jaw seems to stick out past his top one.

That bottom jaw is very strong. If a bulldog bites something, it can lock its jaw in place and it won't let go. In fact, you can lift his whole body off the ground and swing him around but he won't let go and you can't shake him loose. He won't give up.

Some people don't give up easily either. When George Washington was leader of our forces during the Revolutionary War, the first battle went badly. But he didn't give up and finally our nation won its freedom.

Sometimes the Christian life is hard. We may be tempted to give up trying to serve God and to just go along with the world.

But our verse today tells us to be faithful all our lives—until we die—and God will give us the crown of eternal life.

CHALLENGE: If you are tempted to "give up," think of the bulldog and hang on.

44. *DIAMOND CUTTING*

SCRIPTURE: Hebrews 12:1-11

> *My son, do not regard lightly the discipline of the Lord, nor lose courage when you are punished by him. For the Lord disciplines him whom he loves, and chastises every son whom he receives. Heb. 12:5, 6*

Do you collect rocks? When you walk along the shore of a lake or ocean, you may find beautiful stones. The waves have washed the stones up and down over other rocks and sand. This constant rubbing and washing has worn the stone so smooth that the grain found in the inside can be seen. It was the rubbing and the wearing that gave the rock its polish.

In 1905 Captain Wells found the world's largest diamond in South Africa. But it needed to be cut before its real beauty could be seen. In 1908 it was cut by J. Asscher in Amsterdam and set in the British Royal Sceptre as a gift to the King of England from the country of Transvaal in South Africa.

A diamond in the rough, is a diamond sure enough. But it takes grinding and cutting and polishing to bring out the beauty in stones and gems.

The Bible says that God sends troubles, trials, disappointments and hardships into the lives of His children. These hardships cut off the jagged corners of our self-will. They polish our weak faith and make us more dependent on Him. They grind away our selfishness and make us better Christians.

THOUGHT: We don't like to be sanded and polished by God but we must be if we want to shine like strong Christians.

45. *UNDERWATER DANGER*

SCRIPTURE: Luke 6:43-49

> *. . . out of the abundance of the heart his mouth speaks. Luke 6:45*

Icebergs are found in the oceans that are near the North and South Pole. Usually icebergs are formed when large ice floes break up and huge pieces float out to sea. One Arctic ice island was 200 feet thick and covered 140 square miles. It was first noticed in 1946 and finally broke up in 1963. Many chunks must have cracked off and floated away during that time.

The tallest iceberg ever recorded was found off the coast of Greenland. Five hundred fifty feet showed above the water. But the part above the water is not the dangerous part. Scientists say that the part below the water is ten times larger than the part above. The great ocean liner *Titanic* ran into the underwater part of an iceberg and sank with about a thousand people on board. They should have been concerned about the part they couldn't see.

We are a lot like icebergs. Part of us shows—our deeds—our words. But the really important part—our thoughts—can't be seen. They are always known by God for He doesn't look on the outward appearance, but at the heart.

The ice that is above the water and the part that is below is all part of the same iceberg. So a person who speaks angry words does so from a heart filled with anger. A person who speaks kind words does so from a heart filled with kindness. Like an iceberg, there's much more hidden than what shows.

PRAYER: Let the words of my mouth and the meditation of my heart be acceptable in Thy sight, O Lord, my rock and my redeemer. Amen.

46. *LONG OR SHORT*

SCRIPTURE: Luke 18:9-14

> *. . . every one who exalts himself will be humbled, but he who humbles himself will be exalted. Luke 18:14*

Webster's Third International Dictionary has 450,000 words listed in it. The longest one is PNEUMONOULTRAMICROSCOPICSILICOVOLCANOCONIOSIS.

Can you say it? It is the name of a lung disease that miners sometimes have.

Just because something is the longest or the largest doesn't always make it the most important. The Pharisee who thought he was so great and so good came to the temple to pray. The publican also came and brought his humble prayer. It was the unimportant publican who received forgiveness.

Short words can be even more important than the longest one in the dictionary. How about the words in these lists?

Love	Obey	Do
God	His	Unto
And	Law	Others
Others		As
		You
		Wish
		Them
		To
		Do
		Unto
		You.

CHALLENGE: Think of a small but important way to say "Thanks" to Jesus today.

47. *ONE OAR WON'T DO*

SCRIPTURE: Psalm 127

Unless the Lord builds the house, those who build it labor in vain. Unless the Lord watches over the city, the watchman stays awake in vain. Psalm 127:1

A rowboat has two oars. To make the boat move ahead you need to pull both oars at once. If you pull on only one oar, the boat moves in a circle and really doesn't get any place.

The Christian life has two oars too—Work and Prayer.

If you have a problem that needs to be solved and you only pray about it, you are just pulling on one oar.

If you have a task to do and you try to do it all by yourself without praying for God's help, again you are pulling on only one oar.

Work and pray. Pray and work. They go together if your Christian life is going to go toward the goal instead of just in circles.

CHALLENGE: Work as though everything depended on you. Pray as though everything depended on God.

48. THE COW AND THE STUMP

SCRIPTURE: Proverbs 16:1-11

All the ways of a man are pure in his own eyes, but the Lord weighs the spirit. Commit your work to the Lord, and your plans will be established. Prov. 16:2, 3

A farmer put a halter on his cow and led her out of the barn. He used a twenty-foot rope and tied her to a stump so she could eat the clover in the corner of his farmyard.

As the cow began to eat, she walked in a circle. Her rope got shorter and shorter until she could hardly graze at all.

The stump didn't wind up the rope, the cow did it herself. But the cow felt like kicking the stump or at least blaming it for her problem.

Sometimes we behave like the cow did. We make our own problems. Then we like to blame them on someone else—our parents, our brothers, or sisters.

What we did may seem right to us. We hate to admit that we're wrong.

It takes a great deal of honesty to admit we caused our own problem. Yet that kind of honesty is the first step in "unwinding" what went wrong. Only when the cow turns around and walks the other way will she be free of the stump.

CHALLENGE: If you are the cause of a problem, for yourself or for someone else, admit it and start over.

49. CURING THE HICCOUGHS

SCRIPTURE: John 10:7-15

But Jesus said to him, I am the way, and the truth, and the life; no one comes to the Father, but by me. John 14:6

How do you cure the hiccoughs? Maybe you have had to try many things—like holding your breath for a minute, or drinking a glass of cold water, or having someone scare you.

Jack O'Leary of Los Angeles had the longest attack of hiccoughs on record. They lasted from June 13, 1948, to June 1, 1956. During that time he "hicked" about 160,000,000 times and his weight fell from 138 to 74 pounds. People sent him over 60,000 suggestions for cures. But suggestions for cures don't always work.

People have also suggested lots of ways the world could have come into being. They have suggested dates when the world was supposed to end.

Man has made many gods: but Deuteronomy 6:4 says, "Hear, O Israel: The Lord our God is one Lord."

Many religions have suggested ways for man to save himself. Other religions suggest that there are many roads to heaven and any one of them will do.

Jesus tells us that these ideas are all wrong.

THOUGHT: There are many suggestions to help you get over the hiccoughs, but there is only ONE WAY to heaven.

50. *TRY A TELESCOPE*

SCRIPTURE: Psalm 147:1-11

> . . . *He determines the number of the stars, he gives to all of them their names. Ps. 147:4*

At night when the sky is clear, you can look up into the sky and see hundreds of stars. The Bible tells us in Genesis 1:16 that "God made the stars also." Adam and Eve were the first people to see the stars.

Abraham saw these same stars. When God gave Abraham the covenant, He asked him to count the stars if he could and promised, "So shall your descendants be."

David studied the stars when he was a boy tending his father's sheep. Later in Psalm 8 David praised God for the stars: "When I look at thy heavens, the work of thy fingers, the moon and the stars which thou hast established; what is man that thou art mindful of him?"

The wise men in the East saw a special star—the one that led them to Bethlehem, the birthplace of Jesus.

In 1609 Galileo first used the telescope to study the stars. By putting two lenses made of glass together in a special way, he found he could see much farther. Since that time, larger and larger telescopes have been made. The largest telescope in the world is located in a valley in the mountains of Puerto Rico and has a reflecting mirror 1000 feet across.

Through our space explorations and through our scientific instruments, we can know much more about the stars than Adam or Eve, or Abraham, or David, or even the wise men. Do you think we praise God more for those stars?

CHALLENGE: Notice the stars, study them carefully, and PRAISE their MAKER!

51. *THUMBPRINTS TELL*

SCRIPTURE: Daniel 6:5-13

> *You shall not follow a multitude to do evil; . . .*
> *Exod. 23:2*

The FBI has on file in Washington D.C. the fingerprints of millions of people. They are useful to prove the innocence of a person when he is suspected of committing a crime. They can be used as strong evidence if the person is guilty.

Look at the "prints" on your thumb. Do you have a single swirl to the left? a single swirl to the right? a double swirl? You can study your thumbprint by covering it with ink from a ball point pen and pressing it against a clean sheet of paper.

When you touch a glass, a door handle, or anything, you leave your fingerprints.

One thing you can be sure of, your fingerprints stand for you. No one else has prints just like them. You are an individual. Even though you like to do many things with your family and friends, you must still make most of life's most important decisions by yourself.

It's so easy to go with a crowd; to do what others are doing and even daring you to do with them. It takes a lot of courage to stand by yourself and to do what's right. But it can be done—Daniel did it, Noah did it, Martin Luther did it. You can do it too.

THOUGHT: If you find yourself being carried along with a crowd to do something wrong, STOP! Remember your thumbprint. Make your own decision.

52. LONG FINGERNAILS

SCRIPTURE: Daniel 4:28-35

At the end of the days, I, Nebuchadnezzar, lifted my eyes to heaven, and my reason returned to me, and I blessed the Most High. . . . Dan. 4:34

Look at your fingernails. It takes about 125 days for a fingernail to grow from the small half moon at the bottom to the end where it can be cut. A Chinese priest once let his grow for 27 years. His fingernails were 22¾ inches long!

Long ago King Nebuchadnezzar had a dream about a great tree that reached to heaven. It provided a nesting place for the birds and shade for the cattle. But the tree was to be cut down and after seven times had passed, it would be restored again. Only Daniel could interpret the dream. He said the tree stood for the king.

One day when King Nebuchadnezzar was on the palace roof he looked over the city and said, "Is not this great Babylon, which I have built by my mighty power . . ." and then God made the dream come true. The king was driven out to live with the beasts, his hair grew like eagle feathers and his fingernails like bird claws.

Later, when God restored the kingdom to him, Nebuchadnezzar was humble instead of proud. He knew it was not his own power but God who made him king.

THOUGHT: If you are tempted to be proud, or to brag about how great you are, look at your fingernails. Think of King Nebuchadnezzar.

53. *GOD'S BALANCES*

SCRIPTURE: Daniel 5:5-7, 24-30

And this is the writing that was inscribed: Mene, Mene, Tekel, and Parsin. Dan. 5:25

King Belshazzar was terribly frightened when he saw the fingers of a hand write a message on his palace wall. He grew pale and his knees shook. The king couldn't read what it said. He called all his wise men to help but they also were unable to read it. Then the queen remembered Daniel who had interpreted the dreams of the King's father.

Daniel interpreted the handwriting on the wall. It was not a happy message. It said that King Belshazzar's kingdom would end. It would be given to others. He was weighed in the balances and found wanting.

Balances are used by scientists to weigh things carefully. The object to be weighed is placed on one side and a weight, like a one-pound block, is placed on the other. If the object is too light, it goes up. When each side weighs exactly the same, the scale is balanced.

In God's balance of judgment, He puts the law we are to obey on one side, and He puts us, one at a time, on the other side. And since we have disobeyed God's law, we too are "found wanting." But Jesus gets on the scale with us. His perfect obedience fills our need. With Him on our side, the scale balances just right.

PRAYER: Thank you, Lord Jesus, for filling the law for me and bearing the punishment for my sin. Help me to show my thanks to You today. Amen.

54. MAN'S BEST FRIEND

SCRIPTURE: Luke 16:19-31

Truly, I say to you, as you did it to one of the least of these my brethren, you did it to me. Matt. 25:40

Do you have a dog? Or maybe a puppy? If you have ever had a dog, you know what a good friend a dog can be. He follows you everywhere you go. He plays with you every chance he gets. He keeps watch when you are asleep.

Dogs have often saved the lives of people by barking when a house caught fire and everyone was asleep. St. Bernard dogs have saved the lives of persons lost in a snowy blizzard. A sheep dog is very useful to his master. Huskies help the Eskimo people by pulling dog sleds with heavy loads of supplies over the snow fields. Dogs are often companions to people who live alone.

Jesus told a parable about a lonely poor man named Lazarus. He would get the food that fell from a rich man's table. The rich man could easily have helped Lazarus, but he didn't.

Who were Lazarus' friends? Only the dogs. They came and licked his sores.

Finally both the rich man and Lazarus died. Lazarus went to heaven, but the rich man went to hell. Then he wanted God to send Lazarus to put a little cold water on his tongue. But God said, "You didn't care about Lazarus when you were alive, now he can't come to you." It was too late.

THOUGHT: When you see a dog following someone, think of the rich man and Lazarus. Don't wait until it is too late to help others.

55. BEARS AND BOYS

SCRIPTURE: II Kings 2:23-24

> *Honor your father and your mother, as the Lord your God commanded you; that your days may be prolonged, and that it may go well with you. . . . Deut. 5:16*

Bears don't see very well; they are usually nearsighted. They can't hear very well either. But they have a keen sense of smell. They can usually smell someone before they can hear or see him.

When the prophet Elisha was going from Jericho to Bethel a group of boys came out of the city and made fun of him by shouting, "Go up, you bald head! Go up, you bald head!"

God caused two bears to come out of the woods. Forty-two of the boys were torn by the bears because they had not honored or respected the prophet. They poked fun at him.

Jesus showed us how to honor our parents by the way He honored Joseph and Mary. They had taken Jesus to Jerusalem to celebrate the Passover when He was twelve years old. Later they found Jesus in the temple with the Jewish leaders. He went back to Nazareth with Joseph and Mary and was obedient to them.

What you do to show that you honor your father and mother depends on many things. It depends on if you live in the city or the country. It depends on if you are old or young. But whatever your age is, or wherever you live, you must begin by respecting and obeying them.

PRAYER: Lord, help me to be thankful for the parents You have given me. Help me to love and honor them in Your Name. Amen.

56. *SAMSON'S SECRET*

SCRIPTURE: Judges 16:16-31

And he told her all his mind, and said to her, "A razor has never come upon my head; for I have been a Nazirite to God from my mother's womb. If I be shaved, then my strength will leave me, and I shall become weak, and be like any other man. Judg. 16:17

When Hans Langseth died in 1927 he had a beard 17½ feet long. His beard is now preserved in the Smithsonian Institute at Washington, D.C. The longest moustache was grown by Uttar Pradesh between 1942 and 1962. It was 102 inches from one side to the other. A leader of the Thurai monastery in India had hair 26 feet long in 1949.

Before Samson was born, an angel spoke to his parents. Samson was to be a Nazarite. He might not drink any strong drink or get his hair cut. His long hair would show that he was a special servant to do God's will.

As long as he was faithful to God, God gave him great strength. He killed many Philistines with the jawbone of a donkey. He killed a lion with his bare hands. He carried the gates of a city to the top of a hill. He caught 300 foxes.

But Samson was not faithful to God. His friend Delilah pestered Samson until he told her why he was so strong. While Samson slept, Delilah cut his hair. Then God's power left Samson. It was God's power, not Samson's long hair, that made Samson strong. If he had stayed loyal to God, he could have done much more good for God's people Israel.

PRAYER: Help me to be loyal to you, Lord, so that I may be useful in Your kingdom.

57. WATCH YOUR SPEED

SCRIPTURE: Proverbs 28:19-28

A miserly man hastens after wealth, and does not know that want will come upon him. Prov. 28:22

Do you have a speedometer on your bicycle? If not, have you ever ridden alongside of someone who has? How fast can you go? Fifteen miles per hour? Twenty? Twenty-five? If you have a ten-speed, you could probably reach forty miles per hour, especially if you were going down hill.

Going fast on your bike is great if you are in a safe place. But if you go too fast in the wrong place, speed can be dangerous. It can cause serious accidents. Speed can wreck your bike and may hurt you as well.

In the Book of Proverbs, King Solomon tells us to slow down about something. He tells us not to hurry to get rich quickly. Can you think of reasons why this is wise advice?

If a person tries to get rich quickly he may become dishonest. He may steal from someone. He may take advantage of someone else, or cheat. It isn't wrong to get rich. God wants us to work honestly for our riches. He doesn't want us to work so hard to get things that we don't have time or energy left to think about God. He wants place-number-one in our hearts.

THOUGHT: Working for your possessions in an honest way is like riding your bicycle at a safe speed.

58. A PERFECT MEMORY BANK

SCRIPTURE: Revelation 20:12-15

And the dead were judged by what was written in the book by what they had done. Rev. 20:12

A computer can work arithmetic problems much faster than the smartest math teacher can. It has a great mechanical brain that can add or subtract, multiply, or divide long numbers in a split second.

Today's business world uses giant computers for many things. They are used on election nights to count the votes. The ticket salesman at the airport can tell if all of the seats on a certain flight between two cities are sold simply by asking the computer. Computers are important parts of space flight programs. In seconds they compute adjustments needed to correct a swerving from a planned flight path.

Computers have memory banks. Many facts about a person can be fed into a computer: where and when a person was born, where he went to school, what jobs he has held, his Social Security number, all about his income tax reports, and many other things. It remembers things that the person himself may have forgotten. But a computer can remember only what someone has fed into its memory bank.

The Bible tells us that one day we will all gather before the great judgment seat of Christ. At that time nothing will be forgotten. Everything we have done and every word we have said will be made known. How wonderful to know that we have a judge who is also our Savior, Jesus Christ!

PRAYER: Help us today, Lord Jesus, to do the things and say the words that we will not be ashamed of on the judgment day.

59. TANGLING WITH AN OCTOPUS

SCRIPTURE: Luke 22:54-62

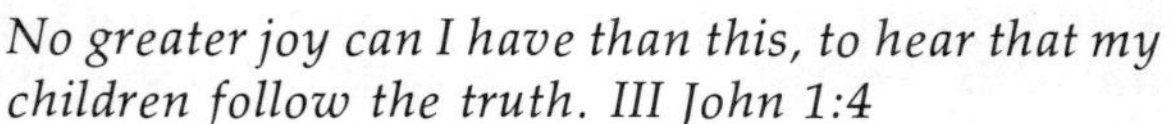

No greater joy can I have than this, to hear that my children follow the truth. III John 1:4

An octopus usually has eight arms or tentacles that branch out in all directions from the central body or eye. Each tentacle has two rows of strong suction cups with which it can cling to an object. When the octopus captures its prey, its glands send out a poisonous substance that paralyzes its victim.

If the octopus thinks danger is near, it gives off an inky fluid that darkens the water. He can then get away unharmed.

Some of the largest species of octopuses have arms up to 28 feet long. They can be very dangerous to a deep-sea diver. First one tentacle could reach out from behind a rock and hold his ankle; then another might encircle his arm, and with his other tentacles the octopus could completely entangle the diver's body and air hose.

Telling a lie is like getting tangled up with an octopus. If you tell one lie to your parents about something, usually you have to tell a second lie to cover up the first one. Then you have to tell another to make the story seem true. Soon you are all wound up in lies and you can't get free.

THOUGHT: When you are tempted to tell a lie, think of the octopus; don't get tangled up.

60. SMILES OF JOY

SCRIPTURE: Luke 15:3-7

A glad heart makes a cheerful countenance, but by sorrow of heart the spirit is broken. Prov. 15:13

Look at your face in a mirror. Do you look happy or sad? It takes more muscles to frown than to smile. When you wear a smile, it shines out to brighten the lives of everyone you meet.

If an apple is half ripe, one boy may say that it is half red already, another may say it is still half green. If the lawn is half cut, one boy may say, "I'm half finished!" while another may grumble, "I still have half to mow!"

Looking at the dark side can be a habit. Looking at the bright side can be a habit too.

The Bible tells Christians to be joyful—when we have little or when we have much; when we are sick or when we are well—even when we are persecuted for something we didn't do.

The angels sang, "Joy to the world!" when Jesus was born. They still rejoice in heaven when a sinner repents. Our joy will be perfect when we too get to heaven.

Paul wrote to the Philippian Christians (4:4) "Rejoice in the Lord always; again I will say, Rejoice!"

PRAYER:

Good morning, Lord,
Thank you for this beautiful new day
Thank you for loving me.
Thank you for saving me.
Thank you for the joy of salvation;
  Make me glad, not sad.
Help me to share my gladness, my jo
  With my family,
  With everyone I meet today.
    Amen.